LILY GREENE

GLOBAL SALAD DELIGHTS

EXPLORING UNIQUE FLAVORS WITH EASY RECIPES FROM AROUND THE WORLD

DJTS PUBLISHING

DJTS Publishing
info@djts-publishing.com

ISBN Ebook: 978-3-910634-03-9
ISBN Paperback: 978-3-910634-04-6
ISBN Hardcover: 978-3-910634-05-3

Imprint: DJTS Publishing

Disclaimer
Please note the information contained within this document is for informational and entertainment purposes only. All effort has been executed to present accurate, up to date, and reliable, complete information. No warranties of any kind are declared or implied. Readers acknowledge that the author is not engaging in the rendering of legal, financial, medical or professional advice. Publisher and Author accept no responsibility or liability for any errors, omissions or misrepresentations expressed or implied, contained herein, or for any accidents, harmful reactions, or any specific reactions, injuries, loss, legal consequences, or incidental or consequential damages suffered or incurred by any reader of this book The content within this book has been derived from various sources. This is not professional advice and this book is no substitute for direct expert assistance, please consult a licensed professional before attempting any techniques that might be outlined in this book.

By reading this document, the reader agrees that under no circumstances is the author responsible for any losses, direct or indirect, which are incurred as a result of the use of the information contained within this document, including, but not limited to, — errors, omissions, or inaccuracies.

The publisher and author are grateful for any suggestions for improvement or advice on possible errors.

TABLE OF CONTENTS

TABLE OF CONTENTS

INTRODUCTION

Hello and welcome to my cookbook, "Global Salad Delights"! My name is Lily Greene, and I am thrilled to be sharing my passion for cooking with you through this book.

Salads are often overlooked as a main dish or even as a side, but they can be so much more than just lettuce and dressing. With this cookbook, I want to show you how salads can be exciting and bursting with flavor. I have traveled all over the world and have been inspired by the unique ingredients and flavors that each country has to offer. This cookbook is a collection of some of my favorite salad recipes that are easy to make at home.

One of the things I love about salads is their versatility. They can be a side dish, a main course, or even a snack. And with this cookbook, you'll never run out of ideas for your next salad creation. Each recipe is packed with bold flavors and interesting textures that will tantalize your taste buds.

Don't worry, this cookbook isn't just for health nuts. While salads are certainly a healthy meal option, my focus is on flavor first and foremost. I believe that food should be enjoyed and savored, not just consumed for its nutritional value. So, whether you're looking for a light lunch or a hearty dinner, these salads won't disappoint.

The recipes in this cookbook cover a wide range of global cuisines including Asian, Mediterranean, South American, and more. You'll find everything from classic Caesar salad to spicy Thai beef salad to refreshing watermelon feta salad. Each recipe includes easy-to-follow instructions and simple ingredients that can be found at any grocery store.

I also wanted to make sure that this cookbook was accessible to everyone regardless of their skill level in the kitchen. Whether you're an experienced cook or just starting out, these recipes are designed to be approachable and easy to follow.

I am confident that you will love this cookbook because it offers something for everyone. Whether you're looking for a light lunch or a hearty dinner salad, there is a recipe here that will satisfy your cravings. And with the variety of global flavors showcased in these dishes, you'll never get bored of eating salads again! Let's explore unique flavors together and discover how delicious healthy eating can truly be.

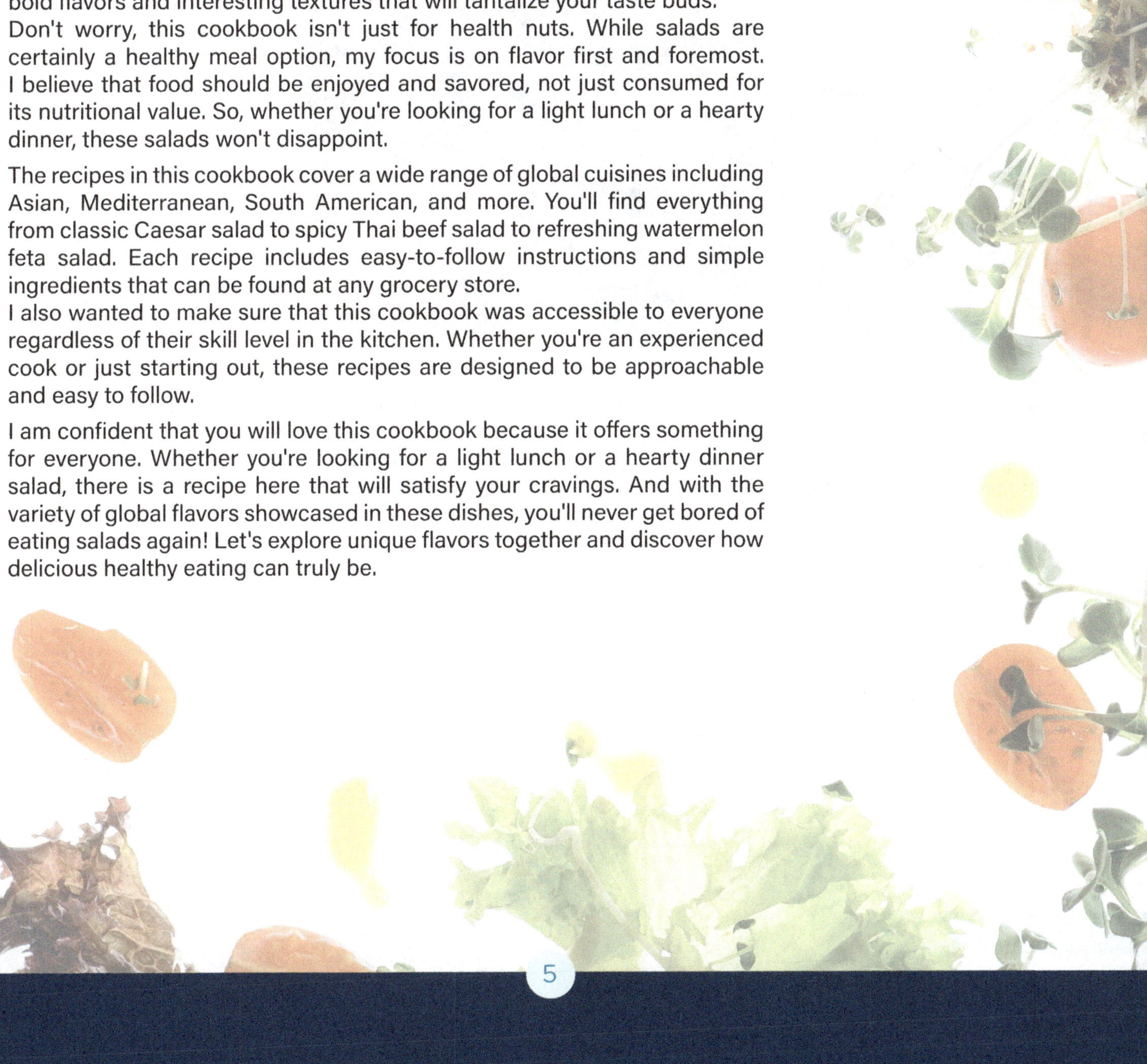

ITALIAN RADICCHIO AND ORANGE SALAD

Preparation Time
10 min

Cooking Time
00 min

Total Time
10 min

INGREDIENTS

- 1/4 cup of chopped walnuts
- 2 tbsp of extra-virgin olive oil
- 1 tbsp of apple cider vinegar
- salt and pepper, to taste
- 1 large head of radicchio, washed and chopped
- 3 oranges, peeled and segmented

DIRECTIONS

1. In a large mixing bowl, combine the chopped radicchio and orange segments. Set aside.
2. In a bowl, stir together the olive oil, apple cider vinegar, honey (or maple syrup), salt, and pepper.
3. Pour the dressing over the radicchio and orange mixture and toss to coat.
4. Sprinkle chopped walnuts over the top of the salad.
5. Serve and enjoy!

SERVINGS: 4

THAI PAPAYA SALAD

Preparation Time
15 min

Cooking Time
00 min

Total Time
15 min

INGREDIENTS

- 1 small tomato, finely chopped
- 1 small cucumber, peeled and cut into small pieces
- 1 small papaya, peeled and cut into small pieces
- 1 green chili, finely chopped
- 1 small red onion, finely chopped
- juice of 1 lemon
- salt to taste
- fresh coriander leaves for garnish

DIRECTIONS

1. Combine the papaya, cucumber, red onion, tomato, and green chili in a mixing bowl.
2. Add the lemon juice and salt. Mix well.
3. Garnish with fresh coriander leaves and serve chilled.

SERVINGS: 4

PERSIAN QUAIL SALAD WITH RASPBERRY DRESSING

Preparation Time
15 min

Cooking Time
00 min

Total Time
15 min

INGREDIENTS

- 2 cups mixed salad greens
- 1/2 cup sliced strawberries
- 1/4 cup sliced almonds
- 4 cooked quails, deboned and sliced
- 1/4 cup olive oil
- 2 tbsp raspberry vinegar
- 1 tbsp Dijon mustard
- salt and pepper, to taste

DIRECTIONS

1. Mix the mixed salad greens, sliced strawberries, almonds, and quails in a large bowl.
2. To make the dressing, combine the olive oil, raspberry vinegar, Dijon mustard, salt, and pepper in a small bowl.
3. Pour the dressing well over the salad, then gently mix to incorporate.
4. Serve without delay.

SERVINGS: 4

GREEK SALMON SALAD WITH LEMON DRESSING

Preparation Time	Cooking Time	Total Time
15 min	00 min	15 min

INGREDIENTS

- 1/2 cup sliced cucumbers
- 2 cups mixed salad greens
- 1/4 cup olive oil
- 1 lb cooked salmon, flaked
- salt and pepper, to taste
- 2 tbsp lemon juice
- 1 garlic clove, minced
- 1/4 cup chopped fresh dill

DIRECTIONS

1. Mix the mixed salad greens, sliced cucumbers, chopped dill, and flaked salmon in a large bowl.
2. To prepare the dressing, whisk the olive oil, lemon juice, garlic, salt & pepper in a small bowl.
3. After pouring the dressing over the salad, carefully stir the ingredients together.
4. Serve right away.

SERVINGS: 4

JAPANESE SESAME CUCUMBER SALAD

Preparation Time
10 min

Cooking Time
05 min

Total Time
15 min

INGREDIENTS

- 2 medium cucumbers, thinly sliced
- 2 tbsp sesame seeds
- 2 tbsp rice vinegar
- 1/2 tsp grated ginger
- 1/4 tsp salt
- 1/4 tsp black pepper

DIRECTIONS

1. In a dry skillet, toast the sesame seeds over medium heat until lightly golden brown and fragrant, about 2-3 minutes. Remove from heat and let cool.
2. Mix the sliced cucumbers and toasted sesame seeds in a large bowl.
3. Whisk together the rice vinegar, grated ginger, salt, and black pepper in a separate small bowl to make the dressing.
4. Pour the dressing over the cucumber and sesame mixture and toss until evenly coated.
5. Allow the salad to rest for at least 10 mins to allow the flavors to meld.
6. Serve and enjoy!

SERVINGS: 4

CHESAPEAKE BAY SALAD

Preparation Time	Cooking Time	Total Time
15 min	00 min	15 min

INGREDIENTS

- 2 ripe avocados, diced
- 1 grapefruit, peeled and segmented
- 6 cups mixed greens
- salt and pepper to taste

For the dressing:

- 3 tbsp extra-virgin olive oil
- 2 tbsp fresh grapefruit juice
- 1 tsp Dijon mustard
- 1 minced clove garlic
- salt and pepper to taste

DIRECTIONS

1. Combine the mixed greens, diced avocado, and grapefruit segments in a bowl.
2. Mix the olive oil, grapefruit juice, Dijon mustard, garlic, salt & pepper in a small bowl with a whisk to make the dressing.
3. Pour the dressing well over the salad and gently toss to cover.
4. Serve right away.

SERVINGS: 4

MEDITERRANEAN BUCKWHEAT SALAD

Preparation Time	Cooking Time	Total Time
10 min	20 min	30 min

INGREDIENTS

- 1 ½ cups grape tomatoes
- ½ cup red onion, diced
- ¼ tsp sea salt
- ½ lemon, juiced
- 1 ½ cups water
- ½ cup feta cheese, cubed
- 2-3 tbsp fresh parsley or mint, chopped
- ¾ cup buckwheat, uncooked
- 3 tbsp olive oil
- 1 ½ cups mini cucumbers, sliced
- ¼ tsp ground black pepper

SERVINGS: 4

DIRECTIONS

1. Rinse the buckwheat and place it in a small saucepan. Add water and a pinch of salt and boil over high heat. Turn to lower the heat to low, cover, and simmer for 15 to 20 minutes. Allow it to sit for 5 mins before fluffing it with a fork. If the water has not all been absorbed, drain the buckwheat in a colander. Set it aside and let it cool completely.
2. Transfer the cooled buckwheat to a large mixing bowl or serving bowl. Add all the remaining ingredients, and toss to combine. If necessary, season with more salt and pepper.
3. Serve with more parsley or mint (optional).

GARDEN SALAD

Preparation Time	Cooking Time	Total Time
15 min	00 min	15 min

INGREDIENTS

- 1 head romaine lettuce, chopped
- 3 radishes, thinly sliced
- 1 medium carrot, julienned or shredded
- ¼ red onion, thinly sliced
- ½ cup seasoned croutons
- 1 cup grape tomatoes, halved
- 1 Persian cucumber, sliced
- 1 cup purple cabbage, chopped
- ¼ cup salad dressing

DIRECTIONS

1. Combine romaine lettuce, cabbage, grape tomatoes, radishes, carrot, cucumber, and red onion in a medium mixing bowl or serving plate.
2. Pour salad dressing on top and toss to combine. Top with croutons and serve.

SERVINGS: 4

STRAWBERRY SPINACH SALAD

Preparation Time
10 min

Cooking Time
00 min

Total Time
10 min

INGREDIENTS

- 2½ cups strawberries, sliced1/2 cup chopped walnuts
- 6 cups fresh spinach leaves
- 1/4 cup balsamic vinaigrette dressing

DIRECTIONS

1. In a bowl, combine the spinach, strawberries, and walnuts. Toss with the balsamic vinaigrette dressing.
2. Serve immediately.

SERVINGS: 2

CLASSIC CALIFORNIAN COBB SALAD

Preparation Time
15 min

Cooking Time
00 min

Total Time
15 min

INGREDIENTS

- 8 cups mixed greens
- 4 hard-boiled eggs, chopped
- 1/4 cup red wine vinaigrette dressing
- 4 slices cooked bacon, crumbled
- 1 avocado, chopped
- 1/2 cup cherry tomatoes, halved
- 1/4 cup crumbled blue cheese
- 1/2 cup chopped cooked chicken breast

DIRECTIONS

1. In a large bowl, arrange the mixed greens.
2. Top with the chopped hard-boiled eggs, crumbled bacon, chopped avocado, cherry tomatoes, blue cheese, and cooked chicken breast.
3. Drizzle with the red wine vinaigrette dressing.
4. Serve immediately.

SERVINGS: 4

MEXICAN TEMPEH CHOPPED SALAD

Preparation Time
20 min

Cooking Time
00 min

Total Time
20 min

INGREDIENTS

- 8 cups chopped romaine lettuce
- 1/2 cup crumbled tempeh
- 1/2 cup cherry tomatoes, halved
- 1/4 cup chopped fresh cilantro
- 1/2 cup chopped cucumber
- 1/4 cup chopped red onion
- 1/4 cup chopped avocado
- 1/4 cup lime vinaigrette dressing

DIRECTIONS

1. In a large bowl, arrange the chopped romaine lettuce.
2. Top with the crumbled tempeh, cherry tomatoes, chopped cucumber, chopped red onion, chopped avocado, and chopped fresh cilantro.
3. Drizzle with the lime vinaigrette dressing.
4. Toss the salad until well combined.
5. Serve immediately.

SERVINGS: 4

BRITISH SMOKED SALMON AND POTATO SALAD

Preparation Time
10 min

Cooking Time
20 min

Total Time
30 min

INGREDIENTS

- 1 pound (450g) baby potatoes, washed and halved
- 1/4 cup red onion, thinly sliced
- 2 tbsp capers, drained and rinsed
- 1/4 cup fresh dill, chopped
- 2 tbsp extra-virgin olive oil
- 2 tbsp apple cider vinegar
- salt and pepper, to taste
- 4 oz (113g) smoked salmon, chopped
- 1 tsp Dijon mustard

DIRECTIONS

1. Take the salted water to a boil in a big pot, then add the potato halves. Fork-tender potatoes, reduce heat, and simmer for 15–20 minutes. Remove the water and set it aside.
2. Mix the boiled potatoes, smoked salmon, red onion, capers, and dil in a big bowl.
3. Mix the olive oil, cider vinegar, mustard, salt, and pepper in a small bowl.
4. Pour the dressing over the potato salad mixture and toss to coat.
5. Serve and enjoy!

SERVINGS: 4

ARUGULA, FIG, AND PROSCIUTTO SALAD

Preparation Time	Cooking Time	Total Time
15 min	00 min	15 min

INGREDIENTS

- 4 cups arugula
- 6-8 figs, sliced
- 4 oz (113g) prosciutto, sliced
- salt and pepper, to taste
- 1/4 cup balsamic vinegar
- 1/4 cup extra-virgin olive oil

DIRECTIONS

1. Mix the arugula, figs, and prosciutto in a large bowl.
2. For the dressing, combine the balsamic vinegar, olive oil, salt, and pepper in a medium bowl and whisk to combine.
3. Dress the salad and toss to combine. Serve immediately.

SERVINGS: 4

MEDITERRANEAN GRILLED CHICKEN AND PINEAPPLE SALAD

Preparation Time
15 min

Cooking Time
18 min

Total Time
33 min

INGREDIENTS

- 4 chicken breasts
- 1 pineapple, sliced
- 6 cups mixed greens
- 1/4 cup sesame oil
- 2 tbsp rice vinegar
- 2 tbsp honey
- 1salt and pepper, to taste
- garlic clove, minced
- 2 tbsp soy sauce

SERVINGS: 4

DIRECTIONS

1. Preheat the grill to medium-high heat.
2. Use salt and pepper to season chicken breasts, and grill them for 5 to 6 minutes per side or until cooked through. Reserve to cool.
3. Grill pineapple slices until lightly charred, about 2-3 minutes per side. Set aside to cool.
4. Mix the sesame oil, soy sauce, rice vinegar, honey, garlic, salt, and pepper in a mixing bowl to make the dressing.
5. Arrange the mixed greens on a platter. Slice the chicken and pineapple into bite-sized pieces and add them to the greens.
6. Drizzle the dressing over the salad and sprinkle it with sesame seeds. Serve immediately.

LATIN AMERICAN MANGO AND BLACK BEAN SALAD

Preparation Time	Cooking Time	Total Time
15 min	00 min	15 min

INGREDIENTS

- 1 red bell pepper, diced
- 1 can black beans, rinsed and drained
- 2 tbsp lime juice
- 2 mangoes, diced
- 1/4 cup chopped fresh cilantro
- 1 tbsp olive oil
- salt and pepper, to taste

DIRECTIONS

1. Combine the diced mango, red bell pepper, black beans, and chopped cilantro in a large bowl.
2. To make the dressing, mix the lime juice, olive oil, salt & pepper in a bowl with a whisk.
3. Pour the dressing well over the salad, and then toss it to coat it. Serve right away.

SERVINGS: 4

FRENCH CHICKEN, APPLE, AND CRANBERRY SALAD

Preparation Time
13 min

Cooking Time
12 min

Total Time
25 min

INGREDIENTS

- 4 chicken breasts
- 1/2 cup dried cranberries
- 4 cups mixed greens
- 1/4 cup Dijon mustard
- 1/4 cup honey
- 1/4 cup extra-virgin olive oil
- 1/4 cup apple cider vinegar
- 2 apples, diced
- salt and pepper, to taste

DIRECTIONS

1. Use salt and pepper to season chicken breasts, and grill them for 5 to 6 minutes per side or until cooked through. Reserve to cool.
2. Combine chopped apples, dried cranberries, and mixed greens in a large bowl.
3. To create the dressing, combine Dijon mustard, honey, apple cider vinegar, oil, salt, and pepper in a small bowl.
4. Add the chicken breasts, cut into bite-sized pieces, and let to cool, to the bowl containing the apples and cranberries.
5. Toss the salad with the dressing to coat it. Serve without delay.

SERVINGS: 4

INDIAN POMEGRANATE RAITA SALAD

Preparation Time
10 min

Cooking Time
00 min

Total Time
10 min

INGREDIENTS

- 1/2 cup pomegranate seeds
- 1 small onion, finely chopped
- 1 small tomato, finely chopped
- 1 green chili, finely chopped
- salt to taste
- 1/2 tsp cumin seeds powder
- 1/4 tsp black pepper powder
- fresh coriander leaves for garnish

DIRECTIONS

1. Add the pomegranate seeds, onion, tomato, green chili, salt, cumin seeds powder, and black pepper powder in a mixing bowl. Mix well.
2. Garnish with fresh coriander leaves and serve chilled.

SERVINGS: 4

IRISH CHICKEN SALAD WITH CHERRY TOMATOES

Preparation Time
15 min

Cooking Time
00 min

Total Time
15 min

INGREDIENTS

- 2 cups baby spinach
- 2 cups arugula
- 2 cups cherry tomatoes halved
- 1/4 cup chopped fresh basil
- 1 cooked Chicken fillet, deboned and sliced
- 1/4 cup olive oil
- 2 tbsp red wine vinegar
- 1 garlic clove, minced
- Salt and pepper, to taste

DIRECTIONS

1. Mix the baby spinach, arugula, cherry tomatoes, chopped basil, and sliced chicken fillet in a large bowl.
2. To prepare the dressing, combine the olive oil, red wine vinegar, minced garlic, salt & pepper in a small bowl.
3. Pour the dressing over the salad, then gently mix to incorporate.
4. Serve without delay.

SERVINGS: 4

FILIPINO GUINES FOWL, OLIVE AND ORANGE SALAD

Preparation Time
05 min

Cooking Time
15 min

Total Time
20 min

INGREDIENTS

- 2 guinea fowl breasts
- 1 jar marinated mixed olives
- ½ tsp crushed fennel seeds
- 2 sticks celery, sliced finely
- 2 bunches watercress

DIRECTIONS

1. Preheat oven to 200°C/400°F/Gas Mark 7. Score the skin on the guinea fowl breasts using a sharp knife and lightly season them with salt and pepper.
2. Heat 1 tbsp of the marinade from the olives in a frying pan and put in the guinea fowl skin side down over a moderate heat until the skin becomes crispy. Transfer them into a roasting dish, skins ide up.
3. Mix the crushed fennel seeds with the olives and sprinkle over the meat. Cook in the oven for approximately 12 minutes. Remove from the oven and leave to cool.
4. Thinly slice the meat and place it in a bowl with the olives, celery and 3tbsp of marinade from the olives.
5. Gently toss the watercress and serve immediately.

SERVINGS: 4

POLISH MACKEREL & BEET SALAD WITH CITRUS DRESSING

Preparation Time
15 min

Cooking Time
00 min

Total Time
15 min

INGREDIENTS

- 2 cups mixed salad greens
- 1/2 cup sliced beets
- 1/4 cup sliced red onion
- 1/4 cup sliced almonds
- 1/4 cup olive oil
- 1 lb cooked mackerel, flaked
- 2 tbsp orange juice
- 1 tbsp honey
- Salt and pepper, to taste

DIRECTIONS

1. Mix the mixed salad greens, sliced beets, red onion, almonds, and flaked mackerel in a large bowl.
2. Whisk everything together olive oil, orange juice, honey, salt & pepper in a small bowl to make the dressing.
3. Pour the dressing over the salad, then gently mix to incorporate.
4. Serve without delay.

SERVINGS: 4

MUTTON SALAD WITH MIXED GREENS AND HERBS

Preparation Time
15 min

Cooking Time
40 min

Total Time
55 min

INGREDIENTS

- 1-pound (450g) boneless mutton, cut into bite-sized pieces
- 4 cups mixed salad greens
- 1/4 cup chopped fresh mint
- 1/4 cup chopped fresh cilantro
- 1/4 cup chopped fresh parsley
- 1/4 cup olive oil
- 2 tbsp lemon juice
- 1 garlic clove, minced
- salt and pepper, to taste

DIRECTIONS

1. Set the oven temperature to 350 °F (175 °C).
2. Put the lamb chunks in a single layer in a roasting pan or baking dish. Salt and pepper the surface, then drizzle with olive oil.
3. In a preheated oven, braise the lamb for 30 to 40 minutes or until cooked through and gently browned.
4. While the lamb is cooking, start preparing the sauce. Mix olive oil, lemon juice, minced garlic, salt & pepper in a small bowl to make the dressing.
5. Combine the mixed salad greens, chopped fresh mint, cilantro, and parsley in a large bowl.
6. Remove the cooked lamb from the oven and allow it to cool for a few minutes.
7. Add the cooked mutton to the salad bowl and drizzle the dressing.
8. Toss gently to combine, then serve immediately.

SERVINGS: 4

SOUTH AFRICAN BANANA SALAD

Preparation Time
15 min

Cooking Time
00 min

Total Time
15 min

INGREDIENTS

- 1 apple, cut into small pieces
- 1 small orange, peeled and cut into small pieces
- 1 banana, cut into small pieces
- 1 small pear, cut into small pieces
- 1 small guava, cut into small pieces
- 1/2 tsp powder spice mix
- 1/4 tsp black pepper powder
- salt to taste

SERVINGS: 4

DIRECTIONS

1. In a mixing bowl, combine all the fruits.
2. Add the powder spice mix, black pepper powder, cumin seeds powder, and salt. Mix well.
3. Serve immediately.

THAI GREEN MANGO SALAD

Preparation Time	Cooking Time	Total Time
15 min	00 min	15 min

INGREDIENTS

- 1 small green mango, peeled and cut into small pieces
- 1 small onion, finely chopped
- 1 small tomato, finely chopped
- 1 green chili, finely chopped
- 1/4 tap. black pepper powder
- salt to taste
- fresh coriander leaves for garnish

DIRECTIONS

1. Combine the green mango, onion, tomato, and chili in a mixing bowl.
2. Add the black pepper powder and salt. Mix well.
3. Garnish with fresh coriander leaves and serve chilled.

SERVINGS: 4

AUSTRALIAN ROCKET AND PEAR SALAD

Preparation Time
15 min

Cooking Time
00 min

Total Time
15 min

INGREDIENTS

- 5 oz (150g) rocket leaves
- 1/2 cup olive oil
- 2 ripe pears, sliced
- 1/2 red onion, sliced
- 2 tbsp balsamic vinegar
- salt and pepper to taste

DIRECTIONS

1. Mix the rocket leaves, sliced pears, and red onion in a large salad bowl.
2. Whisk the olive oil and balsamic vinegar together in a small bowl. Add salt and pepper to taste.
3. Pour the dressing well over the salad and mix it gently.
4. Serve right away.
5. Note: This recipe is gluten-free and nut-free.

SERVINGS: 4

RUSSIAN SALAD

Preparation Time
15 min

Cooking Time
15 min

Total Time
15 min

INGREDIENTS

- 4 potatoes, chopped
- 2 carrots, chopped
- 1/2 cup peas
- 1/2 cup corn kernels
- 1/2 cup chopped pickles
- 1/2 cup vegan mayonnaise
- 2 tbsp Dijon mustard
- salt and pepper to taste

DIRECTIONS

1. In a big saucepan of salted water, simmer the potatoes and carrots until tender, about 15 min. Cool.
2. Mix cooked potatoes, carrots, peas, corn kernels, pickles, and ham in a large bowl.
3. Mix mayonnaise and Dijon mustard in a small bowl. Prepare to taste with salt and pepper.
4. Toss the salad lightly with the dressing to mix.
5. Freeze the salad for at least an hour before serving.
6. Serve chilled.

SERVINGS: 4

ITALIAN ANTIPASTO SALAD

Preparation Time	Cooking Time	Total Time
15 min	00 min	15 min

INGREDIENTS

- 5 oz (150g) mixed salad greens
- 1/2 cup cherry tomatoes, halved
- 1/2 cup sliced cucumber
- 1/2 cup sliced bell peppers
- 1/2 cup sliced salami
- 1/4 cup chopped black olives
- 1/4 cup Italian dressing
- salt and pepper to taste

DIRECTIONS

1. Combine the mixed salad greens, cherry tomatoes, sliced cucumber, and sliced bell peppers in a salad bowl.
2. Add the sliced salami and chopped black olives.
3. Drizzle the Italian dressing over the salad and toss gently to combine.
4. Season with salt and pepper to taste. Serve immediately.

SERVINGS: 4

ASTORIAN WALDORF TUNA SALAD

Preparation Time
15 min

Cooking Time
00 min

Total Time
15 min

INGREDIENTS

- 10 oz(280g) tuna, drained
- 1 cup red grapes, halved
- 1/2 cup chopped celery
- 1/2 cup veagn mayonnaise
- salt and pepper to taste
- 2 apples, cored and chopped
- 1/4 cup apple cider vinegar
- mixed salad greens for serving

DIRECTIONS

1. Combine the tuna, chopped apples, halved grapes, and chopped celery in a large bowl.
2. Mix the mayonnaise, apple cider vinegar, honey, salt, and pepper in a small bowl with a whisk to make the dressing.
3. Pour the dressing well over the salad and mix it gently.
4. Serve the Waldorf tuna salad over a bed of blended salad greens.

SERVINGS: 4

LEBANESE FATTOUSH SALAD

Preparation Time
15 min

Cooking Time
10 min

Total Time
25 min

INGREDIENTS

- 2 pita bread
- 5 oz (150g) mixed salad greens
- 1/2 cup chopped tomatoes
- 1/4 cup olive oil
- 1/2 cup chopped red onion
- 1/2 cup chopped parsley
- 1/4 cup chopped mint
- 1/4 cup lemon juice
- 1/2 cup chopped cucumber
- salt and pepper to taste

DIRECTIONS

1. Set the temperature of the oven to 350°F (180°C).
2. Cut the pita bread into small bite-size pieces and spread/ put them on a baking sheet.
3. Bake pita for 10 minutes until golden and crispy. Let cool.
4. Mix mixed salad greens, chopped tomatoes, cucumber, red onion, parsley, and mint in a big bowl.
5. Dressing: Whisk lemon juice, olive oil, salt, and pepper in a small bowl.
6. Pour the dressing well over the salad and mix it gently.
7. Mix the baked pita pieces gently into the salad.put
8. Serve fattoush immediately.

SERVINGS: 4

FRENCH ENDIVE SALAD WITH ORANGE AND AVOCADO

Preparation Time	Cooking Time	Total Time
15 min	00 min	15 min

INGREDIENTS

- 2 heads endive, chopped
- 1 large orange, peeled and chopped
- 1 avocado, peeled and chopped
- 2 tbsp olive oil
- 1 tbsp apple cider vinegar
- salt and pepper to taste

DIRECTIONS

1. In a large bowl, combine the endive, orange, and avocado.
2. Whisk the remaining olive oil, apple cider vinegar, salt & pepper in a separate medium bowl.
3. Pour the dressing well over the salad and mix it up.
4. Serve right away.

SERVINGS: 4

MEDITERRANEAN RADICCHIO SALAD

Preparation Time
15 min

Cooking Time
00 min

Total Time
15 min

INGREDIENTS

- 1 head radicchio, chopped
- 2 tbsp lemon juice
- 1 tsp Dijon mustard
- 1 bulb fennel, thinly sliced
- 2 tbsp olive oil
- salt and pepper to taste

DIRECTIONS

1. In a large bowl, combine the radicchio and fennel.
2. Combine lemon juice, olive oil, Dijon mustard, salt, and pepper in a small bowl.
3. Pour the dressing over the salad and blend with a stir.
4. Serve without delay.

SERVINGS: 4

NORTH AFRICAN GRILLED PEACH SALAD WITH BALSAMIC GLAZE

Preparation Time
15 min

Cooking Time
00 min

Total Time
15 min

INGREDIENTS

- 4 ripe peaches, halved and pitted
- 4 cups mixed greens
- 1/2 cup sliced red onion
- 2 tbsp balsamic glaze
- 2 tbsp olive oil
- salt and pepper to taste

DIRECTIONS

1. Bring a grill or grill pan to a medium-high temperature.
2. The peach halves are brushed with olive oil and grilled for two to three minutes per side until browned.
3. Combine the mixed greens and red onion in a big bowl.
4. Whisk together the balsamic glaze, olive oil, salt, and pepper in the other bowl.
5. Pour the dressing over the salad and blend with a stir.

SERVINGS: 4

VIETNAMESE DUCK SALAD

Preparation Time	Cooking Time	Total Time
15 min	20 min	35 min

INGREDIENTS

- 2 duck breasts, skin removed
- 2 cups mixed salad greens
- 1/2 cup cherry tomatoes, halved
- 1/2 red onion, sliced
- salt and pepper, to taste
- 1/4 cup olive oil
- 2 tbsp balsamic vinegar
- 1/4 cup of chopped fresh herbs (such as mint, parsley, or cilantro)

DIRECTIONS

1. Set the temperature of the oven to 375 °F (190 °C).
2. Salt and pepper the duck breasts before roasting them on a sheet.
3. Roast the duck for 15-20 minutes. After cooling, slice thinly.
4. Mix salad greens, red onion, cherry tomatoes, and fresh herbs in a big bowl.
5. Combine the olive oil and balsamic vinegar in a bowl, then spread it over the salad.
6. Gently incorporate the duck slices into the salad. Serve without delay.

SERVINGS: 4

NEW ZEALAND LAMB SALAD

Preparation Time
15 min

Cooking Time
05 min

Total Time
20 min

INGREDIENTS

- 1 lb boneless lamb leg, sliced into thin strips
- 1/2 red onion, sliced
- 1/2 cup cherry tomatoes, halved
- 2 tbsp lemon juice
- 2 cups arugula
- 1/4 cup chopped fresh mint
- 1/4 cup olive oil
- salt and pepper, to taste

DIRECTIONS

1. Heat a large skillet over medium-high heat. Add the lamb strips and cook for 4-5 minutes or until browned on all sides.
2. Mix the arugula, red onion, cherry tomatoes, and fresh mint in a large bowl.
3. Whisk together the olive oil and lemon juice in a mixing bowl. Season to taste with salt and pepper.
4. Add the cooked lamb to the salad, then drizzle the dressing over everything. Toss gently to combine.
5. Serve immediately.

SERVINGS: 4

ITALIAN ANTIPASTO SALAD WITH MEAT

Preparation Time
10 min

Cooking Time
10 min

Total Time
20 min

INGREDIENTS

- 1/4 lb (110g) sliced deli turkey breast
- 1/4 lb (110g) sliced deli ham
- 1/4 lb (110g) sliced salami
- 1/2 cup sliced roasted red peppers
- 1/2 cup sliced black olives
- 1/2 cup sliced green olives
- 1/4 cup diced red onion
- 8 oz (225g) gluten-free rotini pasta
- 1/4 cup diced celery
- 1/4 cup chopped fresh parsley
- 1/4 cup olive oil
- 1/4 lb sliced provolone cheese
- 1/4 cup red wine vinegar
- 1 tsp dried oregano
- salt and pepper to taste

SERVINGS: 4

DIRECTIONS

1. Cook the pasta per the directions on the package. Rinse with cold water to cool.
2. Mix the spaghetti, turkey, ham, provolone, salami, roasted red peppers, black olives, green olives, red onion, celery, and parsley in a large bowl.
3. Combine the oregano, salt, and pepper in a bowl with olive oil, vinegar, and red wine.
4. Splash the dressing over the salad and toss to distribute evenly.
5. Chill the salad for at least one hour before serving

CARIBBEAN GOAT SALAD WITH MIXED GREENS

Preparation Time
15 min

Cooking Time
05 min

Total Time
20 min

INGREDIENTS

- 1 lb goat meat, sliced into thin strips
- 1/2 red onion, sliced
- 2 tbsp red wine vinegar
- 2 cups mixed salad greens
- 1/2 cup cherry tomatoes, halved
- 1/4 cup chopped fresh parsley
- 1/4 cup olive oil
- salt and pepper, to taste

DIRECTIONS

1. Heat a large skillet over medium-high heat. Add the goat strips and cook for 4-5 minutes or until browned on all sides.
2. Mix the salad greens, red onion, cherry tomatoes, and fresh parsle in a large bowl.
3. Whisk the olive oil and red wine vinegar together in a small bowl. Sprinkle with pepper and salt to taste.
4. Add the cooked goat to the salad, then drizzle the dressing over everything. Toss gently to combine.
5. Serve immediately.

SERVINGS: 4

BRITISH PHEASANT SALAD

Preparation Time
15 min

Cooking Time
20 min

Total Time
35 min

INGREDIENTS

- 2 pheasant breasts, skin removed
- 2 cups mixed salad greens
- 1/2 red onion, sliced
- 1/4 cup chopped fresh thyme
- 1/2 cup dried cranberries
- 1/4 cup olive oil
- 2 tbsp apple cider vinegar
- salt and pepper, to taste

DIRECTIONS

1. Set your oven's temperature to 375°F (190°C).
2. Salt and pepper the pheasant breasts, then put them on a baking sheet.
3. Roast the pheasant for 15-20 minutes. After cooling, slice thinly.
4. Mix the salad greens, red onion, dried cranberries, and fresh thyme in a large bowl.
5. Drizzle the salad with olive oil and apple cider vinegar in a small basin.
6. Add the sliced pheasant to the salad and toss gently to combine. Serve immediately.

SERVINGS: 4

GERMAN GOOSE SALAD WITH BASIL AND SPINACH

Preparation Time
15 min

Cooking Time
15 min

Total Time
30 min

INGREDIENTS

- 1 lb (450g) goose breast, sliced into thin strips
- 1/2 red onion, sliced
- 1/4 cup chopped fresh basil
- salt and pepper, to taste
- 2 cups baby spinach
- 1/4 cup olive oil
- 2 tbsp balsamic vinegar

DIRECTIONS

1. Heat a large skillet over medium-high heat. Add the goose strips and cook for 4-5 minutes or until browned on all sides.
2. Mix the baby spinach, red onion, and fresh basil in a large bowl.
3. To make the dressing, combine the olive oil and balsamic vinegar in a medium bowl and stir until combined. Prepare to taste with salt and pepper.c
4. Add the cooked goose to the salad, then drizzle the dressing over everything. Toss gently to combine.
5. Serve immediately.

SERVINGS: 4

ARGENTINIAN FLANK STEAK SALAD

Preparation Time
15 min

Cooking Time
05 min

Total Time
20 min

INGREDIENTS

- 1 lb (450g) flank steak, sliced into thin strips
- 2 cups mixed salad greens
- 1/4 cup olive oil
- 1/2 red onion, sliced
- 1/2 cup sliced carrots
- 1/4 cup chopped fresh chives
- 2 tbsp rice vinegar
- salt and pepper, to taste

DIRECTIONS

1. Heat a large skillet over medium-high heat. Add the flank steak strips and cook for 4-5 minutes or until browned on all sides.
2. Mix the salad greens, red onion, sliced carrots, and fresh chives in a large bowl.
3. Mix the olive oil and rice vinegar in a small bowl with a whisk. Add salt and pepper to taste.
4. Add the cooked flank steak to the salad, then drizzle the dressing over everything. Toss gently to combine.
5. Serve immediately.

SERVINGS: 4

GERMAN GOOSE SALAD WITH GRAPEFRUIT VINAIGRETTE

Preparation Time
15 min

Cooking Time
00 min

Total Time
15 min

INGREDIENTS

- 2 cups baby spinach
- 2 cups arugula
- 1 large grapefruit, peeled and segmented
- 1/2 red onion, sliced
- 1/4 cup sliced almonds
- 2 tbsp white wine vinegar
- 1 lb cooked goose meat, shredded
- 1/4 cup olive oil
- 1 tbsp honey
- salt and pepper, to taste

SERVINGS: 4

DIRECTIONS

1. Mix the baby spinach, arugula, grapefruit segments, red onion, sliced almonds, and cooked goose meat in a large bowl,
2. To make the vinaigrette, combine the olive oil, white wine vinegar, honey, salt, and pepper in a mixing bowl.
3. Drizzle the vinaigrette over the salad, then toss gently to combine.
4. Serve immediately.

GREEK SALAD

Preparation Time
15 min

Cooking Time
00 min

Total Time
15 min

INGREDIENTS

- 1 medium cucumber, diced
- 1 medium red onion, diced
- 2 medium tomatoes, diced
- 1 green bell pepper, diced
- 1/2 cup sliced Kalamata olives
- 1/4 cup chopped fresh parsley
- 2 tbsp fresh lemon juice
- 2 tbsp extra-virgin olive oil
- 1 tsp dried oregano
- salt and ground black pepper to taste

DIRECTIONS

1. Mix the cucumber, red onion, tomatoes, bell pepper, and olives in a large bowl.
2. Make the dressing in a bowl by whisking the lime juice, olive oil, oregano, salt, and pepper.
3. Toss salad with dressing.
4. On top of the salad sprinkle chopped parsley.
5. Serve right away or refrigerate.

SERVINGS: 4

INDONESIAN GADO GADO

Preparation Time
10 min

Cooking Time
00 min

Total Time
10 min

INGREDIENTS

- 2 cups mixed greens
- 1 cup cooked edamame
- 1/4 cup sliced red onion
- 1/4 cup roasted peanuts
- 1 cup cooked brown rice
- 1/2 cup shredded carrots
- 1/2 cup sliced cucumber
- lime wedges for serving

For the Peanut Sauce:

- 1/4 tsp ground ginger
- 1 tbsp soy sauce or tamari
- 1 tbsp fresh lime juice
- 1/4 cup creamy peanut butter
- 1/4 cup hot water (or more, as needed to thin the sauce)

DIRECTIONS

1. Mix mixed greens, cooked brown rice, cooked edamame, shredded carrots, cucumber, and red onion in a big bowl.
2. Mix peanut butter, soy sauce or tamari, lime juice, maple syrup, and ground ginger in a small bowl to prepare the peanut sauce.
3. and pourable.
4. Mix the salad with the peanut dressing.
5. Top the salad with roasted peanuts.
6. Serve With lime wedges.

SERVINGS: 2

CAESAR SALAD

Preparation Time
10 min

Cooking Time
00 min

Total Time
10 min

INGREDIENTS

For the Salad:

- 1/2 cup gluten-free croutons
- 8 cups chopped romaine lettuce
- 1/4 cup chopped fresh parsley

For the Dressing:

- 1/2 cup vegan mayonnaise
- 2 tbsp fresh lemon juice
- , salt, and black pepper, to taste
- 1 tbsp Dijon mustard
- 1 tbsp capers, drained
- 1 clove garlic, minced

DIRECTIONS

1. In a large bowl, combine the chopped romaine lettuce and gluten-free croutons.
2. Whisk together the vegan mayonnaise, fresh lemon juice, Dijon mustard, capers, garlic, salt, and black pepper in a small bowl to make the dressing.
3. Toss the salad with the dressing to coat it.
4. Sprinkle the fresh chopped parsley over the top of the salad.
5. Serve immediately.

SERVINGS: 2

CAPRESE SALAD

Preparation Time	Cooking Time	Total Time
10 min	00 min	10 min

INGREDIENTS

- 2 tbsp olive oil
- 4 ripe tomatoes, sliced
- 1/4 cup fresh basil leaves, chopped
- salt and ground black pepper to taste
- 1/4 cup balsamic vinegar

DIRECTIONS

1. Put the sliced tomatoes in a pretty pattern on a serving plate.
2. Upon the tomatoes, scatter the chopped fresh basil leaves.
3. Sprinkle the
4. salad with olive oil and balsamic vinegar.
5. Put in a bowl and s
6. eason with salt and freshly ground black pepper to taste.
7. Don't wait around; serve right away.

SERVINGS: 2

THAI CUCUMBER SALAD

Preparation Time
15 min

Cooking Time
00 min

Total Time
15 min

INGREDIENTS

- 1/4 cup chopped fresh cilantro
- 1/4 cup chopped fresh mint
- 1 tbsp toasted sesame oil
- 2 cucumbers, sliced thinly
- 1/2 red onion, sliced thinly
- 2 tbsp rice vinegar
- 2 tbsp lime juice
- 2 tbsp soy sauce or tamari
- 1/4 cup chopped roasted peanuts
- 1 garlic clove, minced

SERVINGS: 4

DIRECTIONS

1. In a large bowl, combine the sliced English cucumbers, sliced red onion, chopped fresh cilantro, chopped fresh mint, and chopped roasted peanuts.
2. In a bowl, whisk together the rice vinegar, lime juice, soy sauce or tamari, maple syrup, toasted sesame oil, minced garlic, and red pepper flakes (if using) to make the dressing.
3. Drizzle the dressing well over the top of the salad and toss to coat.
4. Serve immediately.

JAPANESE HIYASHI CHUKA

Preparation Time
10 min

Cooking Time
10 min

Total Time
20 min

INGREDIENTS

- 1/2 cucumber, julienned
- 1/2 carrot, julienned
- 1/4 cup sliced shiitake mushrooms
- 1/4 cup thinly sliced scallions
- 2 tbsp sesame oil
- 2 tbsp soy sauce
- 1 tbsp rice vinegar
- 1 tbsp honey
- 8 oz (225) gluten-free ramen noodles
- 1/4 cup thinly sliced red cabbage
- 1/4 tsp grated ginger
- 1/4 tsp garlic powder
- 1/4 tsp red pepper flakes

DIRECTIONS

1. Cook the ramen noodles per the package directions, then soak them under cold water and set aside.
2. Dressing: Mix sesame oil, soy sauce, rice vinegar, honey, ginger, garlic powder, and red pepper flakes in a small bowl.
3. Put the cooked ramen noodles in a big bowl and add the cucumber, carrot, red cabbage, scallions, and shiitake mushrooms.
4. Pour the dressing well over the noodles and mix.
5. Divide the noodle salad into four bowls and garnish with fresh cilantro and sesame seeds if desired.

SERVINGS: 4

UKRAINIAN OLIVYE SALAD

Preparation Time
30 min

Cooking Time
35 min

Total Time
1 hr 05 min

INGREDIENTS

- 2 large Yukon potatoes
- 2 large carrots
- 7 eggs
- 8-9 jarred kosher pickles
- 1 Ballpark chicken/pork franks (450g)
- 1 large yellow onion
- 1 canned sweet peas (450g)
- mayonnaise, for dressing
- fresh parsley, dill or scallions for garnish

DIRECTIONS

1. Wash and scrub wash 2 large potatoes and 2 large carrots. Do not peel the vegetables. Place the potatoes and carrots in a medium pot and cover them with water. Take to a boil over medium-high heat, then decrease the stove heat to low. Cook the carrots for 15-20 minutes and remove them from the pot with kitchen tongs or forks. Cook the potatoes for 30-35 minutes, piercing them with a knife to check if they are cooked through.
2. While the veggies cook, boil 7 eggs for 7-8 minutes. In the other medium saucepan, place 1 (15 oz (420g) weight)) package of ballpark franks covered with water. Take to a boil and cook for 2 minutes, then drain once cooked.
3. Let the cooked ingredients cool to room temperature before peeling and chopping. Thinly slice 8-9 kosher pickles from the jar. Chop the pickles and transfer them to a sieve. Set aside to allow the excess liquid to drain. Peel the cooked potatoes, carrots, and eggs, then thinly slice 1 large yellow onion, 15 oz chicken or pork franks, 2 large carrots, 2 large Yukon potatoes, and the boiled eggs. Chop the sliced ingredients and transfer them to a large salad bowl.
4. Squeeze the juice from the pickles with your hands and add it to the salad. This step is important to prevent the salad from becoming too liquid. Rinse 15 oz of canned peas in cold water and add them to the salad. Gently stir the salad with a spoon, breaking up any sticky potatoes. Refrigerate the salad without dressing.
5. Before serving, dress the salad with mayo. This salad can be stored in the refrigerator for up to 5 days.

SERVINGS: 4

MEXICAN & TEXAN TEX-MEX SALAD

Preparation Time
10 min

Cooking Time
10 min

Total Time
20 min

INGREDIENTS

- 1 lb (450g)of white fish, cut into bite-sized pieces
- 1 tsp ground cumin
- 1 tsp garlic powder
- salt and pepper to taste
- 1 tbsp olive oil
- 1 red bell pepper, sliced
- 1 can of black beans, washed and drained
- juice of 1 lime
- 2 tbsp chopped fresh cilantro
- 1 tbsp chili powder
- romaine lettuce or mixed greens, chopped
- 1 green bell pepper, sliced
- 1 small red onion, sliced

SERVINGS: 4

DIRECTIONS

1. Mix the chili powder, cumin, garlic powder, salt, and pepperin a small bowl.
2. In a large non-stick pan, heat the olive oil over moderate heat. Then, sprinkle the fish with the spice mixture. Cook the fish for three to four minutes per side or until it flakes easily with a fork.
3. Combine the cooked fish, sliced bell peppers, red onion, black beans, cilantro, and lime juice in a large bowl. Toss well to combine.
4. Serve the Tex-Mex salad over a chopped romaine lettuce or mixed greens bed.

TURKISH MELON SALAD

Preparation Time
35 min

Cooking Time
00 min

Total Time
35 min

INGREDIENTS

- 1 small honeydew melon, peeled, seeded, and cubed
- 1 tbsp extra-virgin olive oil
- 2 tbsp fresh basil leaves, chopped
- 1 small watermelon, peeled, seeded, and cubed
- 1 tbsp fresh mint leaves, chopped
- 1 small cantaloupe, peeled, seeded, and cubed
- 2 tbsp balsamic vinegar
- salt and pepper to taste

SERVINGS: 4

DIRECTIONS

1. Combine the cubed cantaloupe, honeydew melon, and watermelon in a large bowl.
2. Add the chopped mint and basil leaves and toss well to combine.
3. Whisk the balsamic vinegar, olive oil, salt, and pepper in a small bowl.
4. Drizzle the dressing well over the melon mixture and toss well to coat.
5. Chill the melon salad in the refrigerator for at least 30 minutes before serving.

IRANIAN SHIRAZI SALAD

Preparation Time	Cooking Time	Total Time
15 min	00 min	15 min

INGREDIENTS

- 2 medium cucumbers, diced
- 2 medium ripe tomatoes, diced
- 1 small red onion, diced
- 1/2 cup chopped fresh parsley
- salt and pepper, to taste
- 2 tbsp extra-virgin olive oil
- 2 tbsp freshly squeezed lime juice
- 1/4 cup chopped fresh mint

DIRECTIONS

1. Combine the diced cucumbers, tomatoes, and red onion in a large bowl.
2. Add the chopped parsley and mint, and mix thoroughly.
3. Mix the olive oil and lime juice in a mixing bowl using a whisk.
4. Pour the dressing well over the salad and toss to distribute evenly.
5. Season to taste with salt and pepper.
6. Refrigerate the salad for at least 30 mins before serving.

SERVINGS: 4

GERMAN POTATO SALAD

Preparation Time	Cooking Time	Total Time
35 min	00 min	35 min

INGREDIENTS

- 2 pounds (900g) of baby potatoes, boiled and cut into small cubes
- 1 small red onion, finely chopped
- 1/4 cup extra-virgin olive oil
- 2 tbsp whole-grain mustard
- 2 tbsp apple cider vinegar
- 1/2 cup chopped fresh parsley
- salt and pepper, to taste

DIRECTIONS

1. Combine the diced potatoes, chopped red onion, and chopped parsle in a large bowl.
2. Whisk together the whole-grain mustard, apple cider vinegar, and olive oil in a separate bowl.
3. Toss the potato mixture with the dressing to coat.
4. Prepare to taste with salt and pepper.
5. Cover the salad in the fridge for at least 30 minutes before serving.

SERVINGS: 4

KOREAN SAENGCHAE

Preparation Time	Cooking Time	Total Time
20 min	05 min	25 min

INGREDIENTS

- 2 tbsp sesame oil
- 8 oz (225g) beef sirloin, sliced thinly
- 1/4 cup chopped scallions
- 1 tbsp rice vinegar
- 2 tbsp soy sauce
- 1 tbsp honey
- 1/2 tsp red pepper flakes
- 1 small onion, thinly sliced
- 2 medium carrots, julienned
- 1 small cucumber, julienned

DIRECTIONS

1. Mix the sesame oil, soy sauce, rice vinegar, honey, and red pepper flakes in a bowl.
2. Add the sliced beef to the marinade, toss to coat, and set aside for 10 minutes.
3. Mix the sliced onion, julienned carrots, and cucumber separately.
4. Heat a skillet over medium-high heat. Add the marinated beef until browned and cooked, about 3-4 minutes.
5. Add the cooked beef to the vegetable mixture, and toss to combine.
6. Top with chopped scallions.
7. Cover the bowl and freezer for at least 30 mins before serving.

SERVINGS: 4

JAPANESE WAKAME SALAD

Preparation Time	Cooking Time	Total Time
10 min	00 min	10 min

INGREDIENTS

- 1/2 cup dried wakame seaweed
- 1 tbsp tamari sauce
- 1/4 cup chopped scallions
- 1 tbsp sesame oil
- 2 tbsp rice vinegar
- 1 tsp honey
- 1 small carrot, julienned
- 1 small cucumber, julienned

DIRECTIONS

1. Soak the wakame seaweed in cold water for 10 minutes or until it has re-hydrated.
2. Drain the seaweed and squeeze out any excess water.
3. Whisk together the rice vinegar, tamari sauce, sesame oil, and honey in a bowl.
4. Add the rehydrated wakame, julienned carrot, and cucumber to the bowl, and toss to coat.
5. Top with chopped scallions.
6. Cover the bowl and freeze for at least 30 mins before serving.

SERVINGS: 2

ISRAELI SALAD

Preparation Time	Cooking Time	Total Time
15 min	00 min	15 min

INGREDIENTS

- 2 boneless chicken breasts, cooked and shredded
- salt and pepper, to taste
- 1 small cucumber, diced
- 1 small red onion, diced
- 1 red bell pepper, diced
- 1/2 cup chopped fresh parsley
- 2 tbsp freshly squeezed lemon juice
- 2 tbsp extra-virgin olive oil
- 2 medium tomatoes, diced

SERVINGS: 4

DIRECTIONS

1. Combine the diced tomatoes, cucumber, red onion, red bell pepper, and chopped parsley in a large bowl.
2. Throw the shredded chicken into the bowl and mix it up.
3. Combine the lemon juice and olive oil in a small bowl using a whisk.
4. Pour the dressing well over the salad and toss it to coat it.
5. Salt & pepper to taste.
6. Cover the salad and put it in the fridge for at least half an hour before you serve it.

LEBANON TABBOULEH WITH FISH

Preparation Time	Cooking Time	Total Time
10 min	25 min	35 min

INGREDIENTS

- 2 cups boiling water
- 2 tbsp extra-virgin olive oil
- 1 cup bulgur wheat
- 1/2 tsp salt
- 1 pound (450g) of white fish fillets (such as tilapia or cod)
- 1/4 tsp black pepper
- 2 medium tomatoes, diced
- 1/4 cup chopped fresh mint
- 1 small cucumber, diced
- 1 small red onion, diced
- 1/4 cup freshly squeezed lemon juice
- 1/2 cup chopped fresh parsley
- 2 tbsp coconut oil
- salt and pepper as per taste

DIRECTIONS

1. Put the bulgur wheat in a big bowl and pour the hot water over it. Cover the basin and wait 20 minutes.
2. Fork-fluff bulgur wheat after draining it.
3. Add the olive oil, lime juice, salt, and black pepper to a small bowl and stir to combine.
4. Mix bulgur wheat with diced tomatoes, cucumber, red onion, chopped parsley, and chopped mint.
5. Pour the dressing well over the salad and toss it to coat it.
6. In a large non-stick pan over moderate heat, melt the coconut oil.
7. Add salt and pepper-seasoned fish fillets to the skillet.
8. Cook the fish on each side for 3-4 minutes or until cooked.
9. Serve the fish fillets over the tabbouleh salad.

SERVINGS: 4

WALDORF SALAD

Preparation Time
20 min

Cooking Time
00 min

Total Time
20 min

INGREDIENTS

- 1 cup seedless grapes, halved
- 1/2 cup chopped walnuts
- 1 cup chopped celery
- 1/4 cup raisins
- 2 medium apples, diced
- 2 tbsp freshly squeezed lemon juice
- 1 tbsp maple syrup
- 1/4 cup vegan mayonnaise
- 1/2 tsp salt
- freshly ground black pepper, to taste
- 4 cups mixed greens for serving

DIRECTIONS

1. Combine the diced apples, halved grapes, celery, chopped walnuts, and raisins in a mixing bowl.
2. Whisk together the vegan mayonnaise, lemon juice, maple syrup, salt, and black pepper in a separate mixing bowl until smooth.
3. Pour the dressing over the apple mixture and toss well to coat.
4. Divide the mixed greens among 4 serving plates.
5. Top each plate of mixed greens with the Waldorf Salad mixture.
6. Serve and enjoy!

SERVINGS: 4

FRENCH NICOISE SALAD WITH CHICKEN

Preparation Time
15 min

Cooking Time
25 min

Total Time
40 min

INGREDIENTS

- 4 boneless, skinless chicken breasts
- 1 tbsp dried thyme
- 1/4 cup olive oil
- 1 tsp paprika
- 1/2 tsp salt
- 1/4 tsp black pepper
- 4 cups mixed greens
- 2 cups cherry tomatoes, halved
- 1/2 cup sliced black olives
- 1/4 cup chopped fresh parsley
- 4 hard-boiled eggs, sliced
- 1/2 cup gluten-free croutons
- 1/4 cup gluten-free dijon mustard vinaigrette

DIRECTIONS

1. Preheat oven to 375°F (190 °C)
2. Mix the olive oil, dried thyme, paprika, salt, and black pepper in a small bowl. Brush the chicken breasts with the mixture and place them on a baking sheet.
3. Roast the chicken in the oven for 20-25 minutes or until fully cooked. Set aside to cool.
4. Combine the cherry tomatoes, black olives, and parsley in a large mixing bowl.
5. Slice the cooled chicken breasts and add them to the mixing bowl.
6. Add the sliced hard-boiled eggs to the mixing bowl.
7. Toss everything in the mixing bowl until well combined.
8. Divide the mixed greens among 4 serving plates.
9. Top each plate with the chicken mixture.
10. Sprinkle the gluten-free croutons over each plate.
11. Drizzle each plate with the gluten-free dijon mustard vinaigrette.
12. Serve and enjoy!

SERVINGS: 4

BRAZILIAN HEARTS OF PALM SALAD

Preparation Time	Cooking Time	Total Time
20 min	00 min	20 min

INGREDIENTS

Dressing Ingredients:

- 6 tbsp extra virgin olive oil
- 3 tbsp freshly squeezed lemon juice
- 2 tbsp Dijon mustard
- 4 large garlic clove pressed or finely minced
- ½ tsp kosher salt
- ¼ tsp freshly ground black pepper

Salad Ingredients:

- 2 hothouse cucumbers
- 1 pound (450g) ripe sweet cherry or grape tomatoes halved
- 2 can or jar (390g each weight) artichoke hearts in water
- 2 cans (1390g each weight) whole hearts of palm
- 2 ripe but firm avocados
- Salt and crushed black pepper to taste

SERVINGS: 6

DIRECTIONS

1. Whisk the olive oil with lemon juice, Dijon mustard, garlic, salt, and black pepper in a small bowl to make the dressing.
2. In the other large bowl, combine the diced cucumbers, halved tomatoes, artichoke hearts, and sliced hearts of palm.
3. Drizzle the lemon oil dressing over the salad and gently toss to ensure everything is coated. Add the diced avocados and gently toss again, taking care not to mash the avocado.
4. Season the salad with salt and crushed black pepper according to your taste. You can serve the salad immediately or cover and refrigerate it until you're ready to serve.

SPANISH ASADILLO MANCHEGO

Preparation Time
5 min

Cooking Time
9 min

Total Time
14 min

INGREDIENTS

- 1 red pepper/capsicum
- 2 medium tomatoes, halved
- 2 cloves garlic, skin left on
- 1 tsp olive oil
- ¼ tsp ground cumin
- ½ tbsp olive oil
- sea salt
- 1 boiled egg, optional

SERVINGS: 2

DIRECTIONS

1. Preheat your oven to 400F (200°C). Cut the peppers/capsicums in half, remove the seeds and stems, and place them cut-side down on a baking sheet. Put halved tomatoes (cut side up) and unpeeled garlic cloves on the baking sheet.
2. Drizzle 1 teaspoon of olive oil over the peppers and tomatoes. Roast in the oven until the peppers' skins blacken and blister, which should take around 8 minutes. Then remove the baking sheet and cover the peppers with clingfilm. Let them cool for about half an hour.
3. Once cooled, peel the peppers/capsicums and transfer them to a blender or a mixing bowl (if using a hand blender). Add the tomatoes, peeled garlic, a pinch of cumin, and a generous pinch of salt, and blend until the mixture is chunky.
4. Pour the mixture into a serving dish and drizzle over ½ tbsp olive oil. Slice the hardboiled egg and arrange it on top of the dish. Serve the roasted pepper and tomato dip with crusty bread on the side.

GREEK QUINOA SALAD

Preparation Time	Cooking Time	Total Time
15 min	15 min	30 min

INGREDIENTS

- 1 cup quinoa, rinsed
- 2 cups water
- 15 oz (425g) chickpeas, drained and rinsed
- 1 red bell pepper, chopped
- 1 yellow bell pepper, chopped
- 1/2 cup chopped red onion
- 1/2 cup chopped fresh parsley
- 1/4 cup chopped fresh mint
- 1/4 cup chopped fresh cilantro
- 1/4 cup chopped walnuts
- 1/4 cup lemon juice
- 2 tbsp olive oil
- 1 tbsp Dijon mustard
- 1 tbsp honey
- 1 clove garlic, minced
- 1/2 tsp salt
- 1/4 tsp black pepper

SERVINGS: 4

DIRECTIONS

1. In a medium pot, boil quinoa and water. Lower heat to medium and simmer until water is absorbed and quinoa is cooked for about 15 minutes.
2. Combine cooked quinoa, chickpeas, red and yellow bell peppers, red onion, parsley, mint, cilantro, and walnuts in a large bowl.
3. Mix lemon juice, olive oil, dijon mustard, honey, garlic, salt, and black pepper in a separate bowl to prepare the dressing.
4. Drizzle the dressing well over the salad and toss until everything is evenly coated.
5. Serve and enjoy!

COSTA RICAN ARUGULA SALAD

Preparation Time
15 min

Cooking Time
00 min

Total Time
15 min

INGREDIENTS

- 1/2 cup cherry tomatoes, halved
- 1/2 cup thinly sliced red onion
- 1/4 cup sliced kalamata olives
- 6 cups arugula
- 1/2 tsp salt
- 1/4 tsp black pepper
- 1 garlic clove, minced
- 1/4 cup olive oil
- 2 tbsp balsamic vinegar
- 1 tbsp Dijon mustard

DIRECTIONS

1. Combine the arugula, cherry tomatoes, red onion, and kalamata olive in a large salad bowl.
2. Whisk the olive oil, balsamic vinegar, dijon mustard, minced garlic, salt, and black pepper until well combined.
3. Pour the dressing well over the salad, and then toss it to coat it.
4. Serve and enjoy!

SERVINGS: 3

MEXICAN TACO SALAD

Preparation Time
15 min

Cooking Time
10 min

Total Time
25 min

INGREDIENTS

- 1½ pound (675g) of ground beef
- 10 oz (280g) nacho-flavored tortilla chips, coarsely crushed
- 1½ cups shredded cheddar cheese
- 1 medium head iceberg lettuce
- 4 cups grape tomatoes, halved
- 16 oz (450g) kidney beans, rinsed and drained
- 2 oz (56g) sliced ripe olives, drained
- 1 large sweet onion, chopped
- 1/3 cup sugar
- 4 oz (113g) chopped green chiles
- 1½ cups Thousand Island salad dressing
- 2 envelopes of taco seasoning divided
- 1¼ cups salsa

DIRECTIONS

1. Cook beef with 1 envelope and 2 tablespoons taco seasoning in a Dutch oven over medium heat until no longer pink; drain.
2. Combine the lettuce, chips, tomatoes, beans, olives, cheese, onion, chiles, and meat mixture in a large serving bowl.
3. Combine the salad dressing, salsa, sugar, and remaining taco spice in a small bowl; pour over the salad and toss to coat.

SERVINGS: 3

ROASTED BROCCOLI SALAD

Preparation Time
15 min

Cooking Time
10 min

Total Time
25 min

INGREDIENTS

- 1 large head of roasted broccoli
- lemon zest from one lemon
- 1/4 cup sliced almonds, toasted
- 10 kalamata olives, sliced in half

Maple Mustard Seed Dressing

- 1 tsp whole grain mustard
- 2 tbsp fresh lemon juice
- 1 tsp fresh tarragon
- 1/8 tsp sea salt
- 1 tsp shallots, minced
- 1 tbsp olive oil
- 1/8 tsp black pepper

DIRECTIONS

1. Roast the broccoli.
2. While broccoli is roasting, make the dressing. Whisk together whole-grain mustard, maple syrup, lemon juice, olive oil, tarragon, shallot, salt, and pepper in a bowl.
3. Cut cooled broccoli into bite-sized pieces.
4. Toss in a bowl with the kalamata olives and half of the dressing.
5. Transfer to a serving bowl. Top with almonds, lemon zest, and feta cheese. Drizzle on more dressing as needed. Serve at room temperature.

SERVINGS: 3

AUSTRALIAN COLESLAW SALAD WITH CHICKEN

Preparation Time	Cooking Time	Total Time
15 min	00 min	15 min

INGREDIENTS

- 1 head of cabbage, finely shredded
- 2 tbsp apple cider vinegar
- 1 red onion, finely chopped
- 2 cups cooked chicken, shredded
- 1/2 cup dairy-free mayonnaise
- 1 tbsp Dijon mustard
- 2 medium carrots, grated
- 1/4 tsp black pepper
- 1/2 tsp salt

DIRECTIONS

1. Combine the shredded cabbage, grated carrots, and chopped red onion in a large bowl.
2. In a separate bowl, whisk together the dairy-free mayonnaise, apple cider vinegar, Dijon mustard, honey, salt, and black pepper until well combined.
3. Pour the dressing well over the cabbage mixture and toss to coat evenly.
4. Put shredded chicken into the bowl.
5. Cover the bowl and fridge for at least 30 mins to allow the flavors to meld together.
6. Enjoy cold!

SERVINGS: 4

BEET SALAD

Preparation Time
10 min

Cooking Time
60 min

Total Time
1 hr 20 min

INGREDIENTS

- 4 medium-sized beets, washed and trimmed
- 4 cups mixed greens
- 1/2 cup sliced red onion
- 3 tbsp red wine vinegar
- 1/2 cup chopped fresh parsley
- 1/4 cup olive oil
- 1 tbsp Dijon mustard
- 1/2 tsp salt
- 1/4 tsp black pepper

DIRECTIONS

1. Set the oven temperature to 400°F. Roast foil-wrapped beets until tender, 55-60 minutes. Peel and cut after cooling. Combine mixed greens, sliced red onion, and chopped fresh parsley in a large bowl.
2. Add the roasted and chopped beets to the bowl. In the other small dish, combine the olive oil, red wine vinegar, Dijon mustard, salt, and black pepper to prepare the dressing. Toss salad with dressing. Serve and enjoy!

SERVINGS: 3

MOROCCAN CARROT SALAD

Preparation Time
10 min

Cooking Time
00 min

Total Time
10 min

INGREDIENTS

- 1 pound (450g) carrots, peeled and grated
- 1/2 cup chopped fresh parsley
- 1/2 tsp paprika
- 1/2 cup chopped fresh cilantro
- 1/4 cup chopped green onions
- 1/4 cup raisins
- 1/4 tsp black pepper
- 1/4 cup olive oil
- 2 tbsp lemon juice
- 1 tsp ground cumin
- 1/2 tsp salt
- 1/4 cup chopped almonds (or pumpkin seeds for a nut-free option)

SERVINGS: 3

DIRECTIONS

1. Mix the grated carrots, chopped parsley, cilantro, green onions, raisins, and chopped almonds (or pumpkin seeds) in a large bowl.
2. Dressing: Mix olive oil, lemon juice, ground cumin, paprika, salt, and black pepper in a bowl.
3. Pour the dressing well over the salad and toss until the items are equally coated.

MEXICAN STREET CORN SALAD

Preparation Time
10 min

Cooking Time
00 min

Total Time
10 min

INGREDIENTS

- 4 cups cooked corn kernels (fresh or frozen)
- 1/4 cup vegan mayonnaise
- 1/4 cup dairy-free sour cream
- 1/4 cup chopped fresh cilantro
- 1/4 cup crumbled cotija cheese
- 1 jalapeño pepper, seeded and minced
- 1 garlic clove, minced
- 2 tbsp lime juice
- 1 tsp chili powder
- 1/2 tsp smoked paprika
- salt and pepper, to taste
- lime wedges and additional cilantro for serving

DIRECTIONS

1. Mix the cooked corn kernels, chopped cilantro, crumbled cotija cheese (or dairy-free cheese), and minced jalapeño pepper in a large bowl.
2. In another small bowl, whisk together the mayonnaise (or vegan mayo), sour cream (or dairy-free sour cream), minced garlic, lime juice, chili powder, smoked paprika, salt, and pepper to make the dressing.
3. Pour the dressing well over the corn mixture and toss until everything is evenly coated.
4. Serve the Mexican Street Corn Salad in a bowl or on a platter, garnished with lime wedges and additional cilantro.

SERVINGS: 4

KOREAN SPICY BEEF SALAD

Preparation Time
10 min

Cooking Time
10 min

Total Time
20 min

INGREDIENTS

- 1 pound (450g) beef sirloin, thinly sliced
- 1/2 cup Korean chili paste (gochujang)
- 2 tbsp soy sauce (or tamari for a gluten-free)
- 1 tbsp sesame oil
- 1 tbsp minced garlic
- 1 tbsp minced ginger
- 2 tbsp vegetable oil
- 4 cups mixed greens
- 1/2 cup sliced cucumber
- 1/2 cup sliced carrot
- 1/4 cup sliced green onions
- 1 tbsp toasted sesame seeds
- lime wedges for serving

DIRECTIONS

1. In a large bowl, mix the Korean chili paste (gochujang), soy sauce (or tamari), sesame oil, minced garlic, and minced ginger to make the marinade.
2. Add the thinly sliced beef to the marinade and toss until evenly coated. Let it marinate for at least 15 mins and up to 1 hour in the refrigerator.
3. In a large non-stick skillet, heat the vegetable oil over high heat. Add the marinated beef and prepare for 3-4 minutes or until browned and cooked.
4. Mix the mixed greens, sliced cucumber, carrot, and green onions in a separate large bowl.
5. Divide the salad mixture among four plates, and top each with the cooked beef.
6. Garnish each plate with toasted sesame seeds and a lime wedge.
7. Serve and enjoy!

SERVINGS: 4

TURKISH SHEPHERD'S SALAD

Preparation Time	Cooking Time	Total Time
15 min	00 min	15 min

INGREDIENTS

- 1 green bell pepper, diced
- 2 tbsp freshly squeezed lemon juice
- 3 medium ripe tomatoes, diced
- 1 medium cucumber, diced
- 2 tbsp extra-virgin olive oil
- 1/2 cup chopped fresh parsley
- 1 small red onion, diced
- 1/4 cup chopped fresh mint
- salt and pepper, to taste

DIRECTIONS

1. Combine the diced tomatoes, cucumber, red onion, and green bell pepper in a large bowl.
2. Add the chopped parsley and mint, and mix everything.
3. With a whisk, combine the olive oil and lemon juice in a small bowl.
4. Drizzle the dressing well over the salad, then toss to coat.
5. Season to taste with salt and pepper.
6. Cover the salad and freeze it for at least 30 minutes before serving.

SERVINGS: 4

THAI MANGO SALAD

Preparation Time	Cooking Time	Total Time
20 min	00 min	20 min

INGREDIENTS

- 1 large Thai green mango or unripe mango
- 1 large red pepper
- A handful of Cos lettuce leaves
- 2 spring onions, white parts sliced finely
- 1 courgette
- 1 red chilli, diced finely
- handful of roasted cashews, chopped
- fresh coriander and/or mint, chopped

Dressing

- 2-3 tbsp lime juice
- 1 tbsp sesame oil
- 1 small garlic clove, pressed
- 2 tbsp tamari (for gluten-free version) or soy sauce
- 1 tsp maple syrup or sugar
- ground pepper, to taste

DIRECTIONS

1. Using a sharp knife or a special peeler, julienne mango, pepper and courgette. Tear Cos lettuce leaves roughly.
2. Whisk all the dressing ingredients together in a small bowl and set aside for the flavours to marry.
3. In a large mixing bowl, mix together all salad ingredients apart from nuts.
4. Mix the dressing in, adjust seasoning. Serve sprinkled with nuts and a few leaves of mint and/or coriander.

SERVINGS: 4

BRITISH PLOUGHMAN'S SALAD

Preparation Time
10 min

Cooking Time
00 min

Total Time
10 min

INGREDIENTS

For the Salad:

- 1/2 red onion, thinly sliced
- 1 cup cherry tomatoes, halved
- 4 cups mixed greens
- 1/2 cucumber, sliced
- 1/2 cup pickles, sliced
- 1/2 cup croutons (use gluten-free bread for a gluten-free option)
- 1/2 cup baked beans, drained and rinsed

For the Dressing:

- 1 tbsp honey (or maple syrup for a vegan option)
- 2 tbsp apple cider vinegar
- 1 tbsp Dijon mustard
- 1/4 cup extra-virgin olive oil
- salt and pepper, to taste

SERVINGS: 4

DIRECTIONS

1. Combine the mixed greens, cherry tomatoes, sliced cucumber, thinly sliced red onion, sliced pickles, baked beans, and croutons in a large mixing bowl. Mix the olive oil, apple cider vinegar, Dijon mustard, honey (or maple syrup), salt & pepper in a bowl.
2. Pour the dressing well over the salad, then toss it to cover it.
3. Serve, and have fun!

JERSEY TOMATO SALAD

Preparation Time	Cooking Time	Total Time
15 min	00 min	15 min

INGREDIENTS

- 4 ripe Jersey tomatoes, sliced
- salt and pepper to taste
- 1/2 red onion, thinly sliced
- 1/2 cup fresh basil leaves

For the dressing:

- 1 tbsp balsamic vinegar
- 1 tsp Dijon mustard
- 1 clove garlic, minced
- 3 tbsp extra-virgin olive oil
- salt and pepper to taste

DIRECTIONS

1. Arrange the sliced tomatoes on a large platter or individual plates.
2. Scatter the sliced red onion and fresh basil leaves over the top.
3. Season with salt and pepper to taste.
4. Whisk the olive oil, balsamic vinegar, Dijon mustard, garlic, salt & pepper in a small bowl for the dressing.
5. Pour the dressing over the salad, and it's ready to serve.

SERVINGS: 6

ITALIAN SPINACH SALAD

Preparation Time	Cooking Time	Total Time
10 min	00 min	10 min

INGREDIENTS

- 6 cups baby spinach leaves, washed and dried
- 1 red onion, thinly sliced
- 2 ripe avocados, diced
- 1 tbsp Dijon mustard
- 1/4 cup dried cranberries
- 1/4 cup sunflower seeds
- 1/4 cup pumpkin seeds
- 1/4 cup olive oil
- 2 medium tomatoes, diced
- 2 tbsp balsamic vinegar
- salt and pepper to taste

DIRECTIONS

1. Combine the spinach, onion, avocado, and tomat in a large bowl.
2. Combine the olive oil, balsamic vinegar, Dijon mustard, salt, and pepper in a mixing bowl.
3. Splash the dressing over the salad and toss to distribute evenly.
4. Sprinkle the dried cranberries, sunflower seeds, and pumpkin seeds over the top of the salad.
5. Serve immediately.

SERVINGS: 4

MALAYSIAN PERCH AND MANGO SALAD WITH LIME DRESSING

Preparation Time
15 min

Cooking Time
00 min

Total Time
15 min

INGREDIENTS

- 2 cups mixed salad greens
- 1 mango, peeled and sliced
- 1/4 cup sliced red onion
- 1/4 cup chopped fresh cilantro
- salt and pepper, to taste
- 1 pound (450g) cooked perch, flaked

Dressing ingredients:

- ¼ cup olive oil
- 2 tbsp lime juice
- 1 garlic clove, minced

DIRECTIONS

1. Mix the mixed salad greens, sliced mango, red onion, chopped cilantro, and flaked perch in a large bowl.
2. For the dressing, whisk the olive oil with lime juice, minced garlic, salt, and pepper in a small bowl.
3. Drizzle the lime dressing well over the salad, then toss gently to combine. Serve immediately.

SERVINGS: 4

CUBAN RAINBOW TROUT AND APPLE SALAD WITH MUSTARD DRESSING

Preparation Time
15 min

Cooking Time
00 min

Total Time
15 min

INGREDIENTS

- 2 cups baby spinach
- 1 apple, cored and sliced
- 2 cups arugula
- 1/4 cup sliced red onion
- 1 tbsp Dijon mustard
- 1/4 cup olive oil
- 2 tbsp apple cider vinegar
- 1 pound (450g) cooked rainbow trout, flaked
- salt and pepper, to taste

DIRECTIONS

1. Mix the baby spinach, arugula, sliced apple, red onion, and flaked rainbow trout in a large bowl.
2. In a mixing bowl, combine the olive oil, Dijon mustard, apple cider vinegar, salt & pepper to prepare the dressing.
3. Pour the dressing over the salad, then gently mix to incorporate.
4. Serve without delay.

SERVINGS: 4

GREEK SARDINE AND CHICKPEA SALAD WITH LEMON VINAIGRETTE

Preparation Time
15 min

Cooking Time
00 min

Total Time
15 min

INGREDIENTS

- 2 cans of sardines, drained
- 2 cups mixed salad greens
- 1 can chickpeas, drained and rinsed
- 1 garlic clove, minced
- 1/4 cup sliced red onion
- salt and pepper, to taste
- 1/4 cup chopped fresh parsley
- 1/4 cup olive oil
- 2 tbsp lemon juice

DIRECTIONS

1. Mix the sardines, mixed salad greens, chickpeas, sliced red onion, and chopped parsley in a large bowl.
2. Whisk together the olive oil, lime juice, minced garlic, salt, and pepper in a small bowl to make the vinaigrette.
3. Drizzle the vinaigrette over the salad, then toss gently to combine.
4. Serve immediately.

SERVINGS: 4

CRAB LOUIE SALAD

Preparation Time
15 min

Cooking Time
00 min

Total Time
15 min

INGREDIENTS

- 6 oz. (170g) vegan crab meat
- 2 cups mixed greens
- 1/2 cup cherry tomatoes, halved
- 1/2 cup cucumber, diced
- 1/2 avocado, diced

For the dressing:

- 2 tbsp vegan mayonnaise
- 1 tbsp ketchup
- 1 tbsp sweet pickle relish
- 1 tsp lemon juice
- Salt and pepper to taste

DIRECTIONS

1. Combine the mixed greens, cherry tomatoes, avocado, and cucumber in a large bowl.
2. Add the vegan crab meat to the bowl and toss gently to combine.
3. Whisk together the vegan mayonnaise, ketchup, sweet pickle relish, lemon juice, salt, and pepper to make the dressing in a small bowl.
4. Drizzle the dressing well over the salad and toss gently to coat.
5. Serve immediately.

SERVINGS: 4

BUFFALO CHICKEN SALAD

Preparation Time
10 min

Cooking Time
25 min

Total Time
35 min

INGREDIENTS

- 4 boneless, skinless chicken breasts
- 8 cups chopped romaine lettuce
- 1 cup sliced carrots
- 1 cup sliced celery
- 1/4 cup dairy-free ranch dressing
- 1/4 cup hot sauce
- 2 tbsp olive oil
- 1/4 cup dairy-free blue cheese dressing
- salt and pepper to taste

DIRECTIONS

1. Set the ovens to 375°F (190°C). Put parchment paper on a sheet pan.
2. Mix spicy sauce and olive oil in a bowl. Salt and pepper the chicken breasts, then brush both sides with spicy sauce.
3. Bake chicken breasts for 20–25 minutes on the prepared baking sheet.
4. Let the chicken cool for a few minutes, then chop it into bite-sized pieces.
5. Combine the chopped romaine lettuce, sliced carrots, and celery in a large bowl.
6. Whisk together the dairy-free ranch dressing and dairy-free blue cheese dressing in a small bowl.
7. Add the chopped chicken to the bowl with the lettuce, carrots, and celery. Pour the dressing well over the top and toss to coat.
8. Serve immediately.

SERVINGS: 4

CHEF SALAD

Preparation Time
15 min

Cooking Time
00 min

Total Time
15 min

INGREDIENTS

- 1 cup sliced cherry tomatoes
- 1 cup cooked and cooled quinoa
- 1/2 cup sliced radishes
- 1/2 cup sliced bell pepper
- 1/2 cup sliced carrots
- 1/2 cup sliced red onion
- 6 cups mixed greens (such as lettuce, kale, and spinach)
- 1/4 cup chopped fresh parsley
- 1/4 cup olive oil
- 2 tbsp apple cider vinegar
- 1 cup sliced cucumber
- 1 tbsp Dijon mustard
- salt and pepper to taste
- 1 cup cooked and cooled chickpeas
- 1/2 cup sliced avocado

SERVINGS: 4

DIRECTIONS

1. Mix the greens, cucumber, cherry tomatoes, radishes, bell pepper, carrots, red onion, and parsley in a large bowl.
2. Whisk together all the olive oil, apple cider vinegar, Dijon mustard, salt & pepper in a small bowl.
3. Pour the dressing well over the salad and toss to distribute evenly.
4. Add the cooked chickpeas and cooked quinoa to the salad and toss to combine.
5. Divide the salad among 4 plates. Top each plate with sliced avocado and crumbled dairy-free cheese, if using.
6. Serve immediately.

APPLE AND PECAN SALAD WITH MAPLE VINAIGRETTE

Preparation Time
15 min

Cooking Time
00 min

Total Time
15 min

INGREDIENTS

- 1/4 cup maple vinaigrette dressing
- 6 cups mixed greens
- 2 apples, cored and thinly sliced
- 1/2 cup chopped pecans

DIRECTIONS

1. In a large bowl, arrange the mixed greens.
2. Top with the sliced apples, chopped pecans, and crumbled blue cheese.
3. Drizzle with the maple vinaigrette dressing.
4. Serve immediately.

SERVINGS: 4

JENNIFER ANISTON SALAD

Preparation Time
15 min

Cooking Time
15 min

Total Time
30 min

INGREDIENTS

- 2 cups chicken or vegetable stock
- 1 cup dry quinoa
- 15oz (425g) can chickpeas, drained and rinsed
- 1 English cucumber, diced
- 1/2 small red onion, minced
- 1/2 packed cup fresh parsley, finely chopped
- 1/2 loosely-packed cup fresh mint leaves, finely chopped
- 1/2 cup roasted salted pistachios, chopped
- 1 cup (4oz) crumbled feta cheese
- salt and pepper, to taste
- For the Lemon Dressing:
- 1/2 cup lemon juice (3-4 lemons)
- 1/2 cup extra virgin olive oil
- 1 Tablespoon honey
- salt and pepper, to taste

SERVINGS: 4

DIRECTIONS

For the Lemon Dressing:

1. Add ingredients to a jar with a tight fitting lid, or small bowl, then shake or whisk to combine.
2. Add chicken or vegetable stock to a small saucepan over high heat then bring to a boil. Add quinoa then turn heat down to low, place a lid on top, and simmer until quinoa is tender and broth has been absorbed, 15 minutes. Fluff cooked quinoa with a fork then scoop into a storage container or large mixing bowl with a lid to cool. Once cool, cover then refrigerate until chilled. Can be done a day or two ahead of time.
3. Add chilled quinoa to a large mixing bowl then add remaining salad ingredients. Drizzle with desired amount of dressing (do not need to use all if you don't want to!) then toss to combine and serve, or refrigerate for up to 3 days.

MEASUREMENT CONVERSIONS

VOLUME EQUIVALENTS (LIQUID)

Standard	US Standard (Ounces)	Metric (Approximate)
2 Tablespoons	1 fl. oz	30 ml
¼ cup	2 fl. oz	60 ml
½ cup	4 fl. oz	120 ml
1 cup	8 fl. oz	240 ml
1½ cup	12 fl. oz	366 ml
2 cups or 1 pint	16 fl. oz	476 ml
4 cups or 1 quart	32 fl. oz	1 L
1 gallon	128 fl. oz	4 L

OVEN TEMPRATURES

Fahrenheit (F)	Celsius (c) (Approximate)
250 °F	120°C
300°F	150°C
325°F	165°C
350°F	180°C
375°F	190°C
400°F	200°C
425°F	220°C
450°F	230°C

VOLUME EQUIVALENTS (DRY)

Standard	Metric (Approximate)
⅛ teaspoon	0.5 ml
¼ teaspoon	1 ml
½ teaspoon	2 ml
¾ teaspoon	4 ml
1 teaspoon	5 ml
1 tablespoon	15 ml
¼ cup	59 ml
⅓ cup	79 ml
½ cup	118 ml
⅔ cup	156 ml
¾ cup	177 ml
1 cup	235 ml
2 cups of 1 pint	475 ml
3 cups	700 ml
4 cups or 1 quart	1 L

WEIGHT EQUIAVALENTS

Standard	Metric (Approximate)
½ Ounce	15 g
1 Ounce	30 g
2 Ounce	60 g
4 Ounce	115 g
8 Ounce	225 g
12 Ounce	340 g
16 Ounce or 1 pound	455 g

 GLUTEN FREE

 VEGAN

 NUT FREE

 DAIRY FREE

Made in the USA
Las Vegas, NV
21 June 2023